Saving Our Sons

Acknowledgements

First and foremost I would like to thank God. In the process of putting this book together I realized how much I thank God for giving me the gift to express myself in words. It is my faith in the Almighty that gives me strength to face challenges and speak truth to power.

To my parents, Daryl and Sharon: Thank you guys for being my parents. I hope I have made you proud. To my Grandmother, Pastor Deloise Chatman, thank you for being my rock and constant source of inspiration. You are my #1 fan and for that I am eternally grateful. If I am blessed to live long enough I pray that I become half the Christian you are. A special thanks to my grandparents, Mr. Jimmie and Ruthie McClendon, thanks for always supporting me and loving me in a special way.

To my siblings: What can I say? You guys are one of the main reasons I strive so hard. I always want to be an example that you can achieve anything in life. I am so thankful that I have you guys in my corner pushing me when I am ready to give up. Special thanks to my aunts and uncles that have pushed me in every endeavor I've set out to achieve. To my many cousins and friends that have pushed me when I wanted to give up. I am forever grateful to my professors and classmates at the ITC that have contributed to my success. Thanks......

There are so many people that have encouraged me during this process in one way or another. I could never call all their names but I send a special thanks to Marquise, Lorenza, Courtney, Latricia, Deion, Gemo, Melanie, Deidra, and Perry. To my Executive team that keeps me focused and balanced, Thanks.... I pray this project effects the lives of young African American boys all over the world..

Foreword

In just a few short weeks I will be moving to the beautiful and sunny capitol city of Tallahassee, Florida and I am filled with both extreme excitement and slight trepidation. Florida is not just a southern state laced with golden beaches, blossoming orange trees, and enviable weather, but it is also the state in which young African American boys are being gunned down as a result of dangerous and recently highlighted *Stand Your Ground* laws. It is a state where as a result of walking down the street wearing a hoodie and carrying a bag of rainbow colored candies, 17-year old Trayvon Martin was shot and killed by a carelessly reckless neighborhood watch volunteer – an episode poignantly addressed by author O'nae Chatman in his opening chapter of *Saving Our Sons* entitled, "What's really going on?"

Relevant, insightful, hopeful, and timely are the words that come to mind when I think of *Saving Our Sons*. Not only does Chatman introduce us to young men whose lives have been snatched from the community way too soon, but he provokes us to consider the seemingly rapid and heartbreaking "devaluation of Black life" that is implied by the treatment of our children across this nation. However, O'nae Chatman does not leave us in a dark space of despair. Rather, Chatman's *Saving Our Sons* presents us with practical and realistic approaches to addressing the physical, emotional, and spiritual needs of the children we love.

Being committed to *saving our sons* himself through speaking, writing, advocacy, and mentorship, O'nae Chatman offers his readers the opportunity and charge to get involved in intentional and meaningful ways – both individually and collectively – to ensure the future successes of our African American young men. Chatman admonishes us to ask the questions: "If not now, when? If not us, who?" As an African American mother of three children, including an 11-year old son, I must do all I can to help our sons see themselves as the brilliant, capable, gifted, talented, radiant souls that they were created by God to be. And, as Chatman reinforces in Chapter 7, "Positive Affirmations," I must take every opportunity that I can to speak life into our sons.

"I am smart… I am worthy… I believe in my abilities… I can do whatever I focus my mind on," are just few of the life-giving affirmations O'nae has used in his own life to inspire himself along the journey. And now, because of *Saving Our Sons*, we are reminded of our collective responsibility to inspire, to guide, to motivate, to parent, to mentor, to influence, to fight for, to protect, to encourage, and to cherish our sons. Thank you, O'nae Chatman, for your gift to humanity in the form of *Saving Our Sons*. I appreciate your labor of love on behalf of our boys!

Dr. Latricia Scriven

Table of Contents

Introduction

Many in America have gone so far as to say black boys in this country have no chance at survival. When you examine the numbers constantly being reported in the news it should cause great alarm. Young black male students have the worst grades, the lowest test scores, and the highest dropout rates of all students in the country. Studies also show that when these young black boys fail in school, they are likely to end up in the criminal justice system.

The Black Star Project reported in a 2013 article, "There are more black men in prisons and jails in the United States (about 1.1 million) than there are black men incarcerated in the rest of the world combined. This should be unacceptable in this country. I believe that action has to be taken immediately if we want to change these statistics. Black men going to prison can no longer be seen as "normal behavior" or business as usual. Saving our Sons is a book dedicated to action and a sustained plan that can help our sons while they are still young, before it's too late. We have stood on the sidelines long enough and watched our sons die. It's time to get in the game. Let's Save Our Sons.

Saving Our Sons
Chapter 1: "What's really going on?"

As I write this book George Zimmerman has just been found not guilty in the murder of Trayvon Martin. Unless you've been living under a rock you've no doubt heard about this trial, one of the most important and televised trials of this 21st century. Social media sites, media pundits, and armchair scholars are all weighing in on the verdict as I pen these lines. As a young black man in America I must admit that while the verdict did not shock me, it did cause me to join the chorus of those that feel justice was certainly not served. Though the Trayvon Martin murder trial has caused much uproar, crimes similar to this murder seem to be on the rise in this country. *The Root* recently issued a 2013 article entitled "Beyond Trayvon:Black and Unarmed." This article discussed the over 20 murders of young unarmed black men at the hands of police officers; those that are supposed to be serving and protecting. As an attempt to honor these young men I took time to list their names and the surrounding circumstances as reported by The Root.

Kimani Gray
Sixteen year old Kimani was shot four times in the front and side of his body and three times in the back by two New York City Police officers as he left a friend's birthday party in Brooklyn on March 9, 2013. The only publicly identified eyewitness is standing by

her claim that he was empty handed when he was gunned down.

Kendrec McDade
Nineteen year old college student McDade was shot and killed in March 2012 when officers responded to a report of an armed robbery of a man in Pasadena, California. He was later found to be unarmed, with only a cell phone in his pocket.

Timothy Russell
Russell and his passenger, Malissa Williams, were killed in Cleveland after police officers fired 137 rounds into their car after after a chase in December 2012. Officers said they saw a possible weapon, but no weapon or shell casings were found in the fleeing car or along the chase route.

Ervin Jefferson
The 18-year-old was shot and killed by two security guards outside his Atlanta home on Saturday, March 24, 2012. Jefferson was unarmed.

Amadou Diallo
In 1999 four officers in street clothes approached Diallo, a West African immigrant with no criminal record, on the stoop of his New York City building, firing 41 shots and striking him 19 times as he tried to escape. They said they thought the 23-year-old had a gun. It was a wallet. The officers were all acquitted of second-degree-murder charges.

Patrick Dorismond
The 26-yar-old father of two young girls was shot to death in 2000 during a confrontation with undercover police officers who asked him where they could purchase drugs. An officer claimed that Dorismond who was unarmed grabbed his gun and caused his own death. The incident made many wonder whether the recent acquittal of the officers in the Amadou Diallo case sent a signal that the police had a license to kill with consequence.

Ousmane Zongo
In 2003 officer Bryan A. Conroy confronted and killed Zongo in New York City during a raid on a counterfeit CD ring with which Zongo had no involvement. The judge in the trial of the officer who shot him (and was convicted of criminally negligent homicide but did not serve jail time) said he was "insufficiently trained, insufficiently supervised and insufficiently led."

Timothy Stansbury Jr
Unarmed and with no criminal record, 19-year-old Stansbury was killed in 2004 in a Brooklyn, N.Y., stairwell. The officer who shot him said he was startled and fired by mistake. Police Commissioner Ray Kelly called his death "a tragic incident that compels us to take an in-depth look at our tactics and training, both for new and veteran officers.' A grand jury deemed it an accident.

Sean Bell

In the early morning hours of what was supposed to be 23-year-old Bell's wedding day, police fired more than 50 bullets at a car carrying him and his friends outside a Queens, N.Y. club in 2006. The three detectives who were charged – one of whom yelled "gun", although Bell was unarmed were found not guilty of all charges.

Orlando Barlow

Barlow was surrendering on his knees in front of four Las Vegas police officers when Officer Brian Hartman shot him in 2003. Hartman was 50 feet away and said he thought the unarmed 28-year-old was reacting for a gun. The deadly shooting was ruled "excusable". But a federal investigation later revealed that Hartman and other officers printed T-shirts labeled "BDRT", which stood for "Baby Daddy Removal Team" and "Big Dogs Run Together", and that they'd used excessive force during two separate investigations.

Aaron Campbell

In 2005 Campbell was shot in the back by Portland, Oregon., police officer Ronald Frashour, who said he thought the unarmed man was reaching toward his waistband for a weapon. Witnesses said the 25-year-old was walking backward toward police with his hands locked behind his hand moments before the fatal shot was fired.

Victor Steen
In 2009, 17-year-old Victor, who was riding his bicycle, refused to stop when chased by a police officer in a cruiser in Pensacola, Florida. In response, the officer aimed his taser out of the driver's window, fired, then ran over the unarmed teen, killing him. The deadly incident was captured on video. A judge ruled that no crime was committed.

Steven Eugene Washington
Washington was shot by gang-enforcement officers Allan Corrales and George Diego in Las Angeles one night in 2010 after he approached them and appeared to remove something from his waistband. The officers said they'd heard a loud sound in the area and the 27-year-old, who was autistic, was looking around suspiciously. No weapon was ever recovered.

Alonzo Ashley
Police say that 29-year-old Ashley refused to stop splashing water from a drinking fountain on his face at the Denver Zoo one day in 2011, then made irrational comments and threw a trash can. The responding officers, who didn't dispute that he was unarmed, killed him with a taser, saying he had "extraordinary strength". No criminal charges were filed against them.

Wendell Allen
Allen was fatally shot in the chest by officers executing a warrant on his house on March 7, 2012, in New Orleans. The 20-year-old was unarmed, and five

children were home at the time of his death. Police found 4.5 ounces of marijuana on Allen after they killed him. An attorney for the family says that New Orleans police are investigating whether Officer Joshua Colclough was wrong to pull the trigger.

Ronald Madison and James Brissette
In 2005, in the aftermath of Hurricane Katrina, five officers opened fire on an unarmed family on the east side of the Danziger Bridge, killing 17-year-old James Brissette and wounding four others. Next, officers shot at brothers Lance and Ronald Madison. Ronald, a 40-year-old man with severe mental disabilities, was running away when he was hit, and was stomped on and kicked by an officer before he died. In a federal criminal trial, five officers involved in what have become known as the "Danziger Bridge Shootings" were convicted of various civil rights violations, but not murder.

Travares McGill
In 2005 in Sanford, Florida (the same county in which Trayvon Martin was killed), the 16-year-old was killed by two security guards, one of whom testified that Travares was trying to hit him with his car. But evidence showed that the bullet that killed the teen hit him in the middle of the back and that the guard kept firing even after the car was no longer headed toward him.

Ramarly Graham

In 2012 Officer Richard Haste shot and killed 18-year-old Graham in the bathroom of his grandmother's Bronx, N.Y., home after a chase while he was attempting to flush a bag of marijuana down the toilet. Police did not have a warrant to enter the house, and Graham had a weapon. A grand jury charged the officer with manslaughter, but a judge tossed out the indictment in May, ruling that the prosecution inadvertently misled jurors by telling them not to consider whether he was warned that Graham had a gun.

Oscar Grant

Oakland, California transit police Officer Johannas Mehserle said that he accidentally used his gun instead of his taser when he shot Grant on a train platform on New Year's Day 2009. The 22 –year-old was lying facedown with his hands behind his back, being subdued by another police officer, when he was killed. Mehserle was convicted of involuntary manslaughter and sentenced to only two years for taking Grant's life. He was released after 11 months.

I'm sure you felt the way I felt after first viewing this list of young men killed senselessly. These types of headlines have become common place around this country. Just tune in to CNN on a weekly basis, you'll discover black people; especially black boys being killed at an alarming rate. Things are happening so fast to our young people that before we get the details of one event, another has happened in the same week. In the wake of these tragedies we are left with the questions, "What's really going on?" Why is this happening to our young people?" What can we do to protect these young people from being sacrificed on the alter of American racism and injustice?"

Black youth in this country are in peril. It seems that countless organizations are searching for answers, strategies, or anything plausible to help save these children. Many strategies have been proposed and even implemented. Some have worked and some have not. Organizations such as National Action Network, Rainbow Push Coalition, NAACP, and others are speaking out. The murder of Trayvon Martin has sparked public debate on the value of black life in this country. The acquittal of George Zimmerman has awakened the community in a way that has not been felt in years. After the not guilty verdict many took to the streets, as well as social media, to raise the pressing questions, "What do I tell my son?" How do I tell my son to react in the fact of injustice?" How do we handle being stereotyped by those that consider us suspicious?" These are just a few of the questions currently being debated on social media. These are important questions that have to be answered by every person that cares about the longevity of our sons. These questions were instantly met by cynicism by those on the right. In an attempt to deflect the obvious racial tension involved in the Zimmerman trial, these pundits begin to ask, "Why are black people not concerned about black on black crime?" This was a total slap in the face to every father, mother, aunt, uncle, sister, brother, and cousin that has experienced the loss of a black child at the hand of another black person. Yes, those in black communities do care about black-on-black crime. Crime of any nature or magnitude is seen as unacceptable by many, as it should be. Any life taken is a tragedy, whether at the hands of a white person, black person or otherwise. Life is valuable. All life is valuable.

From Exodus to America

Exodus 1:15-17 "And the king of Egypt spake to the Hebrew midwives, of which the name of the one was Shiphrah, and the name of the other Puah. And he said, when ye do the office of a midwife to the Hebrew women, and see them upon the stools; if it be a son, then ye shall kill them: but if it be a daughter, then shall live. But the midwives feared God, and did not as the king of Egypt commanded them, but saved the men children alive."

In Exodus Chapter 1, we are given the story of a Pharaoh that rises to power. This Pharaoh notices that the Hebrew people are growing and multiplying in number. As a result he decrees that all "boy" babies be killed as soon as they are born. He gives this order to the Hebrew midwives, or those responsible for helping the Hebrew women deliver their children. These midwives were Godly women that refused to take the life of these baby boys. It is important to note that these women recognized the value of these babies.

They realized that every single child held great importance and significance to God. What if this country had the same reverence and respect for our children today? What if our boys were able to live in a world where they were not demonized and categorized as thugs, gangsters, and hoodlums? This story in Exodus always intrigues me because it is the boys that Pharaoh feared. He feared the boys because he recognized their power and strength. Our boys possess power beyond measure. This power places fear in the heart of those dedicated to seeing them fail. Just as there was a conspiracy to destroy boys in Egypt, I believe there are current day conspiracies to destroy our boys today. Young black males are faced with a magnitude of challenges. It's impossible to discuss black males without highlighting the disproportionate rates of incarceration, school failure, poverty, and the many other issues plaguing our communities. One of the greatest conspiracies in play is the "War on Drugs". This so called war has been going on for years and contributes to the destruction of black males at an alarming rate. Dr. Juwanza Kunjufu states, "Although violent crime in America has steadily declined over the past 20 years, the number of young black males in juvenile detention centers and prison has increased rapidly. Year after year thousands upon thousands boys are carted off to detention centers and adult facilities. Although African American males comprise only 6% of the country's population, they represent over 50% of the penal population. At this time one in three African American males between the ages of 20-29 is either in jail or on probation. The large majority of these young boys being arrested are arrested for drug related crimes." I assert that Pharaoh is still sending out the decree, "kill those boys."

The impact of incarceration on these boys has been devastating. Every young boy that goes to jail represents another life removed from the landscape of the community. Once these young boys have gone to jail and received a record, it becomes increasingly hard to maintain employment once back in society. This especially applies to those young males living in the urban areas where employment is already scarce. Dr. Jonathon Livingston states, "Inequities in sentencing have led to longer jail and prison terms for these young men at the most malleable period in their development. Their re-entry into the community as productive citizens becomes cumbersome, and many find themselves lost and unable to negotiate the demands of the new urban landscape characterized by low wage service labor. Return into the drug trade and life of crime becomes a viable choice for many of these young men, accounting for the high rates of recidivism for young African American males." The call of Pharaoh is still being heard. Can you hear it??

The Impact of Negative Stereotypes

From the time I was a youngster I was always taught that a person was not what they were called, but rather what they answered to. I believe this to be true, however, when you don't know who you are you will answer to anything that you're called. This happens because time has not been taken to find true identity. I believe our young boys have lost their true identity, causing them to acquiesce to terms and definitions put forth by media and other outlets that wish to destroy the image of black males. In other words, there are assumptions that have been placed on our children by the dominant culture. Black males have been painted with a broad brush in most instances. People associate black males with less than flattering images such as laziness, violent tempers, unstable minds, and promiscuity tendencies. These images are damaging to young boys that are still in the stage of figuring out who they are and what their role is in life. These images have become the template of how boys see themselves. Being depicted as a thug and hoodlum constantly by media often causes on to feel that he is a thug, even when he's not. In order to save our sons there must be positive reinforcement on our part. Our boys must be reminded that media does not have the final say over their lives.

How can we instill positive affirmations into these young men?" We certainly cannot continue to let media, trashy reality shows, and misguided politicians tell our boys who they are. It is our job as parents, leaders, teachers, preachers, and mentors to insert positive affirmations and messages into young people, daily. Everyday must be a day filled with love and positive reinforcements. We all have a role to play; our boys are depending on us.

Chapter 2: "The Value of Life

In 2012 columnist Juan William cited a comprehensive study by the Justice Department in 2005 on the subject that he said should have been a "clarion call" for the black community and nation at large. Williams asserted that almost one half of the nation's murder victims that year were black, and a majority of them were between the ages of 17 and 29. Black people accounted for 13 percent of the U.S. population in 2005. Yet they were the victims of 49 percent of all murders and 93 percent of black murder victims were killed by other black people. Williams highlighted a very poignant point that needs to be addressed. Black on Black crime is a major problem in this country. Our young men are dying at alarming rates at the hands of other black boys. All of this raises key questions that have to be answered. One of these questions is, "What is the value of a black life?" Are our young people's lives as valuable as those of other races and nationalities?" If we are going to save a generation of boys we have to place extreme value on their lives. President Barack Obama made a 2013 speech in which he addressed the George Zimmerman verdict and its implications on the nation. The President was very vigilant in reminding the nation that something needed to be done to reassure African American males that their lives were valuable in this country. The fact that such a statement and speech had to be made speaks volumes to us. This country is still lacking in its efforts of making people of color feel valuable.

For many young men of color, defying the system or going against societal norms has become a way of protesting against a system that shows them no love. Many are doing things such as wearing saggy pants as a way of rejecting a society that has rejected them. Our boys are valuable even if they are not able to rap, dance, or dribble a basketball. Imagine growing up in a society that declares you worthless and guilty before your true character is ever assessed. That's a shame!!!!

Devaluation of Black Life

One of the major problems facing black boys and black men is the notion that life in general is disposable. Just watch the nightly news show. The devaluation of life is blatantly obvious. Anytime death of our children is seen as "normal behavior" something is wrong. It should never be "business as usual" when children are slain in the street. It's heartbreaking to see people simply brush off the value of black life in this country. Yes, that goes for black people that do it as well. Institutional racism has left those in Black America in a very dangerous place. Shanell Matthews states it brilliantly in a recent article. "With a maternal and fatal mortality rate higher than any other race (often caused by stress brought on by racial burdens), Black mothers often experience traumatic birthing experiences that include forced cesareans, trivializing attitudes by medical professionals, and contemptuous care that has led to death or serious injury. If they survive this, black children are given the least resources, have the least access to healthcare, endure some of the most toxic and contaminated environments, and deal with structural and interpersonal racism throughout adolescence and into adulthood, where they risk the chance of being shot to death by people like George Zimmerman."

People seem to have little sympathy or empathy for those that live in communities that don't look like theirs. Every child deserves respect regardless of their color. Safety and security should not just be for the rich and famous. It should become a reality for all children. With the death of Trayvon Martin, and the miscarriage of justice in this case, the devaluation of black life is evident. I look forward to a day when the media circuits put forth a concerted effort to call out the continued emphasis placed on the marginalization of the black family.

We Have to Speak Out

In the previous section I talked about this country not valuing the lives of black boys. We are all familiar with this lack of care and concern on part of those in the larger society. However, I would be remiss and disingenuous if I did not call out our own communities into action as well. We can no longer afford to let our boys see us kill each other like animals. Since I have relied heavily on the Trayvon Martin story in this book, I think I need to point out another angle through which we should see the case. There was heavy outrage after George Zimmerman was found "not guilty" of murdering Trayvon Martin. The question I want to raise is, "When will we become just as outraged when a black person takes the life of another black person?" Have we begun cheapening our own lives? How does cheapening affect our boys? Why are we silent about injustice done to us by those in our own communities? The slaughter of our black men and boys should never be met with silence. Part of this silence is seen in our "no snitching" campaigns within our neighborhoods. When we know someone that has taken the life of another young person and we say nothing about it, we have become part of the problem. We should be marching and having rallies for those slain at the hands of black people, not just when they are slain by a racist white person. We can't allow ourselves to ever become desensitized to young people being killed. In other words, people within our communities have to know that the killing of our boys is unacceptable and will not be tolerated, regardless of whether the killer is black, white or any race. It should not take media coverage to galvanize us into action. We have to start speaking out. Our sons are depending on us.

Chapter 3: Saving Our Sons through Education

While pursuing my Masters Degree at the Interdenominational Theological Center, my thesis project was entitled "Teaching Our Sons: The Effects of Afro-Centric Pedagogy on African American Boys". This particular project provided me with many twist and turns. There were things I discovered while completing this project that further informed the gross negligence I had assumed concerning education. The most startling thing I discovered was that very little if any African American history was being taught in the school system. As I raised this concern, my professor reminded me that things had not changed in the many years since I had attended high school. The major part of my project was spent interviewing teachers, principles, and other administrators in some of the schools located in Atlanta Georgia. Two of these schools were unique in the fact that they were over 98% African American. As I interviewed staff, I raised questions such as, "Is there any resemblance of an Afro-centric pedagogy taught here, or one that centers the child within his/her own culture?" I quickly learned that the lack of African American History or any history that contributed to the children's self esteem was lacking. Through my research I was able to assert that this was a major problem for our children. It's a fact that the educational system in America is in trouble. This trouble is affecting African American boys at an alarming rate.

Dr. Carter G. Woodson in his classic book, "The Miseducation of the Negro," states it brilliantly by saying "African Americans have been educated away from their own culture and traditions and attached to the fringes of European culture; thus dislocated from themselves."

In 2014 Woodson's words still ring true. It is no secret that the educational system in this country is in dire straits. As usual, the trouble seems to be affecting African Americans the most. The failure of this system as we know it has tremendous impact on the quality of life faced by African American males, particularly as the result of an unsuccessful school experience. It is fact that there is a direct correlation between black boys that perform poorly in school, especially those that choose to drop out, and their involvement in the penal system. Many scholars have written about the vast inequalities in schools, especially those defined along racial lines. "In a nation with the most unequal distribution of wealth and income of any industrialized country, students in high poverty, high minority schools are routinely provided fewer resources, Moreover, these students have less access to experienced teachers, to high quality curriculum, and to advanced level courses than their more affluent white peers. Not surprisingly, they experience lower rates of high school graduation, academic achievement and college attendance levels."

The sad fact is that public policy tends to be the driving force in these inequalities. "Minority students are disproportionately represented among those who are denied diplomas or retained in grade due to the proliferating use of high stakes testing throughout the country. Nationwide, blacks students are nearly three times as likely as white students to be labeled mentally retarded and almost twice as likely to be labeled as having emotional disturbances. Once identified, Black and Latino students are also more likely to be isolated in substantially separate classrooms from their non-disabled peers. Official dropout rates mask a widening "graduation gap" between minority and white students." In our 100 largest cities, 58% or more of ninth grade students in high minority schools don't graduate four years later."

On top of these problems is the "zero tolerance" approach to wrongdoing within the school. This policy leads to a high suspension rate among minority students. Despite the seeming objective neutrality of a policy titled "zero tolerance", the actual operations of school discipline and related systems reveal a host of subjective factors that appear to be a breeding medium for disparities and discrimination. For example, one study found that Black students are punished more severely for lesser offenses, such as disrespect, excessive noise, threat or loitering" than their white peers."

The Proof Is In the Pudding

While doing research I ran across a school that's leading the way in education for African American boys. I highlight this school because it proves that our boys can learn when placed in a school system that cares about their well being. Urban Prep, located in Chicago has created a model that should awaken the entire country. This school for the last 4 years has graduated 100% of its male students, all 100% entering four-year-college/universities. This goes against the argument that all our boys are dead beats, pants sagging thugs. In addition to Englewood, Urban Prep Academies have two additional locations, Bronzeville Campus and West Campus. All three schools are located in predominately African American neighborhoods, where students score lower on standardized test, where nearly half of its teachers quit in three years and where limited resources and materials are hindering a child's opportunity to succeed." At the time of the launch of this school in 2002, the dropout rate for black males in Chicago was 60 percent." How is it that this school has been able to benefit our boys while others have struggled? The creator of Urban Prep put several things in place that led to his school's success.

How it's done

How does a school comprised of all African American boys have a 100% graduation rate? Why is this not making worldwide news? There are key strategies that have been put in place by Urban Prep to assure its success. Let's take a look at these strategies used at Urban Prep.

#1 – Respect: Four elements are introduced to the everyday culture of Urban Prep. The first is respect. Each student is referred to by their surnames. This means that a student is Mr. Smith, Mr. Jones, or Mr. Jackson instead of David, Frank, or Todd. This has proven to create a positive culture based on respect.

#2- Responsibilities: A code of conduct has been established through a strict dress code. Students wear blazers, ties, khakis, and white shirt everyday to school. Everyday these young men are expected to be on time, dressed properly, and ready to adhere to the school code.

#3- Rituals: Everyday at Urban Prep begins with community. The entire school gathers every morning in the gym to acknowledge students that are doing exceptionally well. These students are applauded in front of their peers. College admittance is also congratulated in front of peers. At the end of the gathering all students are required to recite the Urban Prep creed, *"We're college bound"*. We are exceptional not because we say it, but because we work hard at it, we have a responsibility to our family, community and world, we believe!!!

#4-Relationships: Every teacher is responsible for lighting fire under the students. Teachers are given school issued cell phones, and encouraged to call parents about homework and other assignments.

#5-Parental Engagement
Parental engagement is critical and at the top of the list at Urban Prep. Workshops are offered to parents of these students, along with regular meetings, and access to online grades and more.

Somewhere along the way we have bought into what the media is saying about our sons. We need to cut the voice of media down and turn up the voice of our inner spirits. Urban Prep is just one of many schools doing tremendous work with African American boys across the country. We can't give up; our boys are depending on us.

<u>Let's Do the Work</u>
I've pointed out the major obstacles in the educational system; now let's get down to business. What can we do to help our boys?" What can we do to save our sons in the area of education?" I assert that there are strategies that can be implemented in homes, churches, YMCA's, etc. Since we know that many schools are negligent in properly teaching our boys, let's get back to the basics and do what we know to do.
#1 – We must teach responsible behavior and skills
- We must stress "expectation". Children that have no expectation will act as such. Our boys have to be expected to be great. No Mediocrity Allowed!!!

- Our boys must be taught early to respect authority. Lack of respect can no longer be tolerated. Adults must provide the model that these young men are expected to follow. Respect means not exchanging words with adults, learning the basics such as saying, "Yes Sir" and Yes Ma'am". There was a time when youngsters knew not to disrespect adults; let's get back to the basics.

- Our boys must be taught respect for others. Our children have to be taught that every person is valuable and has value. This also means respecting others property.

- Our boys must be taught the value of work. Nothing less than "quality work" will be accepted, at home, school, church, or otherwise. We must teach a spirit of excellence to our young boys.

- We must spend resources investing in our boys. Too many parents are spending countless resources on perfecting their son's sports prowess, but very little is spent on education. Academics have to be first and foremost in the life of every child. This means teaching our boys ownership, not just ways to supply entertainment to others.

- We have to be diligent in making sure that our sons are at the proper reading level by the time they reach third grade(we will discuss this further in a later chapter). Children love to read when they are challenged to do so. Less television, more reading.

- Create a stable home environment that includes positive interaction with a male figure. Positive male mentorship is vital in the life of a young boy.
- Negative media images must not be allowed in the home. Our boys need to see affirmative images that lift their spirits and feed into their creative geniuses.
- Our boys must learn early that respecting women is non-negotiable, it's a must. Disrespect for women cannot be tolerated on any level. Let's do the work.........

Chapter 4: Back To Fundamentals

Studies show that the most important year for a student is third grade. To many this may come as a shock. What is it that makes the third grade so critical? Well, it is critical because the third grade is the year that students move from "learning to read- to reading to learn". "The books children are expected to master are no longer simple primers but fact-filled texts on the solar system, Native Americans, the Civil War, etc." It is at this point that many students begin to fall behind. This fall off for many creates a gap that continues to grow if intervention methods are not incorporated. As you can imagine this critical grade is even more critical for African American children. As time goes on we seem to be losing a generation of boys in the area of education, reading literacy in particular.

Tavis Smiley, in a recent 2012 segment of the Smiley Report issued these chilling facts:

- 54% of African Americans graduate from high school, compared to more than three quarters of white and Asian students.
- Nationally, African American male students in grade's K-12 were nearly 2 ½ times as likely to be suspended from school in 2000 as white students.
- In 2007, nearly 6.2 million young people were high school dropouts. Every student who does not complete high school cost our society an

estimated $260,000 in lost earnings, taxes, and productivity.

- On average, African American twelfth-grade students read at the same level as white eight-grade students.

- The twelfth-grade reading scores of African American males were significantly lower than those for men and women across every other racial and ethnic group.

- Only 14% of African American eighth graders score at or above the proficient level. These results reveal that millions of young people cannot understand or evaluate text, provide relevant details, or support inferences about the written documents they read.

- The majority of the 2.4 million people incarcerated in U.S prisons and jails are people of color, people with mental health issues and drug addiction, people with low levels of educational attainment, and people with a history of unemployment or underemployment.

These facts are chilling and real in every sense of the word. These statistics raise many questions for educators and parents alike. How are the same kids that are happy, enthusiastic, and exuberant about going to school in kindergarten all of a sudden becoming disinterested by third grade? "African American children are only 17% of the total school population in American, yet they represent more than 41% of students in special education, of which 80% are black males." Eighty percent of all students referred to special education are below grade level in reading and writing." Dr. Jawanza Kunjufu describes it this way:

"Schools fail boys in many ways. Not only are they resistant to change, but many programs that are perfect for high energy, right-brain learners, such as physical education and the arts, have been virtually eliminated in schools. Even though girls mature academically at a faster pace than boys, boys are expected to read and master fine motor movements before they are ready. Boys are excellent at doing complicated NBA math, NFL math, rap math, and drug math, yet they are failing basic math and algebra in school."

The fact that our boys are failing at such an alarming rate should be cause for great alarm. I propose that the answer lies in returning back to the basics. The basics are foundational and can be attained through perseverance and hard work.

Let's Read

Studies show that kids spend nearly 55 hours a week watching television, texting, and playing video games. This is unacceptable, especially for kids that are reading below grade level. There is no excuse for parents or guardians that allow children to waste this much time on a weekly basis. The Koiser Family Foundation in 2012 did a study that produced shocking numbers. They reported that kids are working the equivalent of a full-time job consuming media: 7 hours and 38 minutes every day, on average. This should instantly raise red flags to adults. How can we allow brilliant minds to waste so much time in front of a television set, instead of a book. This is simply not good for our children. "Not surprisingly ,reading rates have declined. Kids spend about 25 minutes a day reading books."

This also leads to less time being spent outside, which means less physical activity which leads to obesity at a younger age. This is a problem. We must get our boys reading at an earlier age. This means also guaranteeing that these young students receive the best reading instruction we can give. This instruction is not solely on the shoulders of the school teacher. This responsibility has to start at home.

Strategies

#1 – Allow children to choose a book that they love to read. Students love the opportunity to pick a book that means something to them. This does not mean that the adult should never choose the books. It simply means that at some point the child should be given an option.

#2- Teach accuracy in reading- When we are teaching young people to read we have to make sure that accuracy is the focal point. This means stressing word-recognition so that the child understands the reading passage. Students that lack accuracy usually become frustrated and uninterested.

#3- Read aloud to the child. You should take every opportunity to read aloud to your child. "Listening to an adult model fluent reading increases students own fluency and comprehension skills."

#4- Lets get it done. These strategies will do our sons no good if they are not implemented and put into action. Every exercise is worth the time. Our boys are worth it. Let's get reading!!!!!

Chapter 5: The Alarm Has Sounded

Whenever any major study is being conducted, talked about, or debated, one of the questions that always arises is, "What is the church's role in helping to solve this problem?" If we are going to help a generation of young boys the church has a major role to play. The truth is, the church, more specifically the black church, simply has to use all resources available to gain traction in this struggle. According to Dr. Walter E. Williams in a 2012 article, "Each year, roughly 7,000 blacks are murdered. Ninety-four percent of the time, the murderer is another black person. According to the Bureau of Justice Statistics, between 1976 and 2011, there were 279,384 black murder victims. Using the 94 percent figure means that 262,621 were murdered by other blacks, though blacks were only 13 percent. This is alarming! The church has a role to play in seeing these numbers changed. This means using every resource available to train and teach our young people in the community. This means everyone in the community pitching in and providing help in the problem areas. Every community has a pool of resources that can be tapped into, even if it's very little. Within the community are retired teachers, preachers, writers, medical professionals, and other professionals. We are all needed in the fight to save our sons. It truly takes a village. Do your part.

We Must Do Better

I will never forget talking to a young man that lived in a rough part of Atlanta, GA. While discussing life we discussed a recent murder that had taken place within the city limits. I was shocked to hear that the murder was seen as just "another day in the hood" as he described it. As I began to display my disdain for this lack of concern I realized that some people have simply become desensitized to death and destruction. These things happen so much in our urban centers that it becomes "business as usual" or just "hood politics" of the day. We can no longer stand for the death of our young boys being business as usual. This is a major crisis. We can no longer afford to be passive in the face of destruction in our neighborhoods. It seems that many have simply lost hope and resorted to a feeling of nihilism. Some in our communities have thrown up their hands in despair. Schools seem to be in despair, only giving our boys skills that are short term at best. If our boys continue to die what does it mean for the future of our communities? Who is going to protect our communities and marry our daughters? Who is going to lead strong families and raise strong and conscious children? If teachers are not allowed to teach relevant material in the classroom it is our job to teach our children at home and in the community.

Facing Challenges

Our boys are facing several challenges that should cause great alarm. If the future of young African American boys is going to be bright, changes must be made. As long as imprisonment, murder, and unemployment are in the picture there is yet work to be done. For some young people the mere mention of opportunity seems like something out of reach, something far away or unattainable. These challenges at times seem to be insurmountable. The entire community is responsible for confronting the challenges faced by our young males. Our boys need positive examples, while being encouraged to become all they can be in life. It only takes one look at the news to see why the challenges being faced are so pervasive. Men of color make up 60 percent of the prison population throughout the United States. In 2012 Chicago experienced 508 homicides and over 1,900 shootings. This is shameful. The alarm for organizing and creating special coalitions has been sounded. This fight takes everyone becoming involved and getting their hands dirty in the trenches. The elders have a saying, "it takes a village to raise a child." Not only does it take a village to raise children, it takes a village to protect and propel them to success. African American males have to be informed and equipped for the things they will face. "African American ancestors stood in the gap for their future generations by fighting against slavery, police brutality, racism, and many more problems that the African American community has to deal with during different eras in the United States." It is time that our boys become a major priority on the list of every organization, group, council, coalition, and all other civic establishments. "With all the resources being placed in other areas of great concern, the plight of African American males should be a major priority for the leadership in the United States to consider." The alarm is sounding.

<u>Creating Support Systems</u>

Researchers have found that creating support systems consisting of families, teachers, and peers makes boys more likely to succeed. These support systems help to create an atmosphere in which boys can thrive. When our boys have support and encouragement from those that have their best interest they have a better chance of being successful. One of the greatest strategies I have used is mentoring. Mentoring young people can create very positive results in their lives. There are various organizations that have been created for this very purpose, including Boys and Girls Clubs, Big Brother/Big Sister, 4-H Clubs, YMCA's, and many more. "Studies have found that youth with mentors often feel better about themselves and are less likely to indulge in abusive behaviors." Mentorship is one of the keys to success for our sons. Let's get started.

Chapter 6: Mentoring

"**M**entoring is critical if we intend to address much of the pain, abuse and abandonment that African American males suffer from. While we struggle to find mentors for young African American males, it is equally important to locate the fathers of these young brothers. A young boy's first mentor should be his father and the other men in his family. Responsible fatherhood must be viewed as a necessary action step to begin the healing process among African American males."

Vance Simms
Founder & Executive Director
Father Matters
Phoenix Arizona

It's no secret that mentoring is needed in our communities. I personally believe that mentoring is the single most important part of a young boy's life. When dealing with young boys that have been socially criminalized, marginalized, and demonized, mentoring is needed. I believe there are several ways to help our sons, but none more important than mentoring. Mentoring is of utmost importance because it helps to shape the discussion around the role of youth and adult partnerships. Our young men are in dire need of seeing respectable, responsible adults in the community. These young men need to know that there are other options, ones greater than being pimps, thugs, and drug dealers. They must see alternate realities.

Mentoring deals with an adult or authority figure providing support, guidance, encouragement, and instruction to a protégé. According to the MENTOR/National Mentoring Partnership, nearly 17.6 million young Americans need or want mentoring, but only 3 million are in formal, high-quality mentoring relationships. These numbers should make all of us cringe. These are young people that are being robbed of the chance to see positive examples exemplified. This is a tragedy in my opinion. Some have even raised the question of recruitment for such programs, even the lack of recruitment in general. How can we better recruit qualified mentors?" Do our communities have enough mentors to meet the vast demand?" Have we canvassed every athletic club, every barbershop, every sporting event in the community? There are simply people that do not realize the importance of getting involved as a mentor. Many people see this as the job of parents. I agree that parents should be role models in the home. However, there are broken homes in our communities and someone has to step up and get the job done in these situations. Mentoring does not cost a fortune, only time.

"Based on findings from Fountain &Arbeton, mentoring programs estimated costs range from $1,000 to $1,500 a year per mentor (depending upon the nature of the program). These costs are much lower than intensive remedial programming and more comprehensive service programs. The annual costs for mentoring are considerably lower than the cost of incarcerating one juvenile for a year. Based on data from the Office of Juvenile Justice Delinquency and Prevention, the average amount of money it takes to incarcerate a youth for one year is $43,000. This comes to roughly $117 per day. High-end detention programs costs about $64,000 per year ($175 per day) and low-end programs cost about $23,000 ($63 per day)."

It does not take a rocket scientist to see that mentoring serves as the "best-practice" when it comes to youth. The cost to mentor a child is far less than the cost of incarcerating a child, not even counting the emotional cost on the families of those being incarcerated. Mentoring can be done in a variety of areas, including spoken word, dance, music, and the arts. Since every child has a different and unique learning style there is great flexibility in the way mentoring sessions can be administered. The mentor's job is to help develop the individual both personally and professionally.

Author Mychal Wynn describes it best by saying, "The tragic plight of African American males in regard to low academic performance, high school graduation, and college enrollment together with the increased numbers of juvenile detainees, prison incarceration, and gang involvement requires a strategic response.

African American males mentoring other African American males is one of the critical strategies that is required. In fact, it may be the most important strategy in ensuring the successful development and motivation of young African American males into a generation of men who will be loving fathers to their children, faithful husbands to their wives, and leaders for their community."

Are You Ready

There are several types of mentoring programs that you can become involved in. Personally, I have always been a fan of one-on-one mentoring and group mentoring. One-on-one mentoring requires meeting with the mentee at the most appropriate times and cultivating the mentor-mentee relationship. This includes going over homework, teaching life skills, or just simply talking about things going on in the life of the mentee. One-on-one mentoring can produce very positive results; however, it takes full dedication on behalf of the mentor. The mentor has to take it seriously and make sure that timeliness and goal setting are at the forefront.

Group mentoring can also yield very positive results. This is when an adult works with a small to medium sixed group of young people. This group mentoring model is used frequently in church settings. A lot can be accomplished using this model when the mentor has as outlined and detailed plan.

What's Your Excuse?

I have heard every excuse in the book when it comes to mentoring. The main excuse seems to deal with time. Many people feel that they are just too busy to make an impact on the lives of young people. I encourage these people to reevaluate this time excuse. The time it takes to watch a sporting event is the time it takes to complete a mentoring session with a young person.

Some people feel that they are not qualified to mentor a young person. It does not take an advanced degree to become a mentor. Young people only want to know that you care about them and their well being. You don't have to be rich to be a mentor, nor do you have to be famous. You just have to have a caring heart and the willpower to do so. Young people don't care how much you know until they know how much you care.

The Strategy

Now that I've expressed the importance of mentoring, it is important that we have the appropriate strategies for recruiting the mentors. I am a believer in coming up with practical solutions that can be instantly implemented with hard work and dedication. It does no good to know the problem, but do nothing to come up with a solution. The solution lies in the recruiting process. Let's look at possible ways of recruiting.

Strategies:

#1 – In order to recruit more mentors single mothers have to become our greatest ally. There is nothing more powerful than a mother telling the heartfelt story of her young son's life being impacted through mentoring.

#2- We must have recruiting campaigns that appeal to men. These campaigns should start in the community. The focus should be placed on businesses, professional organizations, and other groups that have men with strong character.

#3- We must use all media outlets willing to help in the recruitment of mentors. This includes using social media tools to recruit as well.

#4- We must get female mentors involved in the recruitment process. It takes a village to help a child.

#5- It is important that coaches, leaders, pastors, and other community leaders are contacted in this effort. These leaders can become "recruitment specialist" in the recruitment process.

#6- Mentors can be recruited from local colleges, allowing students to gain community service hours when available.

Places to recruit:
1. Alumni Associations
2. Churches
3. Universities/Professional Schools
4. Community Organizations
5. Police Departments
6. Barber shop
7. Beauty Shops
8. Fraternities
9. Sororities

10. Book Clubs
11. Sports Teams
12. Business Establishments
13. High Schools
14. Corporations

This list is just a small list of places that we should use to recruit mentors. This list is certainly not the only list we should pull, but it's a starting place. These organizations have traditionally yielded positive recruits. Let's get moving….

Let's Ask Important Questions

Mentoring is important, but asking the right questions is also important. Our sons are plagued with issues that need to be addressed. These issues can be dealt with in a proper manner when they are handled in adequate time. Many young boys are experiencing problems at home, and broken homes can produce broken children in the absence of intervention. It is the mentor's job to talk to the student in a caring manner, or one that allows the mentee the opportunity to express his feelings in a safe environment. A safe environment is vital because trust is of utmost importance in the mentee/mentor relationship. The mentor should be interested in how the student is doing in school, home, and the community in general. The goal is to encourage the mentee to become a positive, focused, and caring individual. Mentors should ask questions such as, "How are you doing in school?" What subjects are your favorite subjects? What subjects are you having problems with? Do you feel safe in your school and home environment? These are just a few of the important questions that need to be asked in the mentoring sessions. These questions will help the mentor to gauge the emotional stability of the mentee. This is important. Every child deserves the opportunity to go to school in a safe environment.

Peer Relationships

While mentoring it is important to take inventory of the peer relationships in which your mentee is involved. These are the people that are closest to your mentee. This is important because the peer group a young boy hangs around can tell you a lot about his behavior. It is important to find out if he is involved in bullying. It is also important to find out if he is being bullied. Bullying is serious and it has to be addressed if your mentee is involved in any way. Assessing your mentee peer relationships can also let you know if he is involved in activity that may be detrimental to his future. In this case it is important that you take the right steps to help the mentee. Let's get started....

Chapter 7: Positive Affirmations

It is no secret that our sons need positive affirmation in their lives. Positive affirmations are defined as "techniques used to program the subconscious mind to effect change by repeating (or meditating on) a key phrase to bring about the desired outcome." This means that every opportunity to speak life into our boys is of the utmost importance. Speaking life is allowing these boys to speak positive messages into themselves throughout the week. These affirmations are important because they influence self-worth and self esteem in positive ways. There are so many messages and images put out on a daily basis that are negative. These negative images are shown throughout the day on television, on social media, and via other outlets.

Over the years I have discovered that using positive affirmations in my speeches to young people has been successful. There are young people that have been told all their lives that they were nothing, no good, and worthless. As a mentor, parent, or community elder it is our job to inform these young people of their importance and worth. I believe that our lives are interconnected and valuable to the overall stability of the community. It's time to speak life to our young men.

<u>Purpose Driven</u>

I believe that every person has a purpose. Involved in this purpose is a process that has to be lived out. It is important that our sons realize their purpose for living. As leaders it is our job to teach young people the importance of seeking God for their purpose. We were created with greatness on the inside. Our sons need to know that they can set goals and reach their full potential. They can have a positive outlook on life, one that propels them to success. It is very discouraging to hear young people say that they were born to hustle and to be involved in illegal activity. God has placed us here to be so much more than hoodlums, criminals, and thugs. Our sons have potential but many times it takes urging from adults to tap into that true potential. We sometimes tap into these things through instruction, direction, and mentoring.

Taking Responsibility
I am a believer in taking responsibility for my actions. As I mentor young people throughout the country I always take time to teach responsibility. Many young people are born into environments that are less than flattering. While living in bleak realities, these young men need to understand that challenges in life can propel them if they refuse to give up. Many of our sons are growing up with no father in the home. Many have absolutely no role models to look up to. Yes, this is terrible, but I often remind these young men that they are still expected to take responsibility for their lives. This means controlling the things that they can control and choosing to achieve in the face of adversity.

When I speak to young people across the country I typically start my speeches off with my personal story. I inform these young people that even though I had challenges growing up, I was still expected to do the important things like read, study, homework, and household chores. Taking responsibility means stepping up to the plate even if you're poor and have limited resources. Let's remind our sons that they can achieve in the face of adversity.

Using What You Have

It is our job to teach our sons the importance of using the gifts they've been given. It does not take a whole lot to genuinely inspire young people to be the very best they can be in life. This includes teaching them about the ups and downs that come in life. We have to expect that mistakes will sometimes be made. It is our job to say, "Don't be afraid. We will help you."

Our sons are talented in a variety of areas, including music, arts, sports, science, mathematics, and others. Many times our young people have no one to help them tap into the gifts they have been given. These gifts must be nurtured through inspiration and guidance by parents, adults, mentors, and other caring individuals. Even gifted children make horrible mistakes when no adult is guiding them in the right direction. Our sons have gifted minds that can be used to help better the community. Let's encourage these boys to use their gifts in the proper manner. Let's inspire.

Self-Motivation

Positive affirmations, in my opinion, are aligned with self-motivation. Adults are responsible for helping in the process of self motivation. This means teaching boys to be proactive in life, while empowering them to be independent. While growing up in rural Mississippi, my grandmother taught me the valuable lesson of being self motivated and independent by assigning me chores. Chores and daily tasks instilled in me the importance of hard work and responsibility. When hard work is expected, it teaches children to respect the things they have, seeing that the things they have are a result of their effort. This is true independence in my estimation. "This simply means that the process of educating our boys requires that we require of them to tackle real life problems and watch them find solutions. They should have early work responsibilities, management responsibilities, and social responsibilities."

As I mentor young men I am always reminded and confronted with the vast potential they possess. Many over the years have viewed potential through only the lenses of sports prowess. Potential goes far beyond sports. As encouragement is given to these young men they begin to discover and realize just how much potential they really have. Dr. Naim Akbar says, "If his energies are only directed towards fun and games, jokes and play, then he continues to recycle in that dimension and there is no growth possible." Self-motivation is important because it teaches our sons that there is more to life than fun and games. Life is about decisions and discipline.

Everyday Motivation

Over the years I have often found strength from quotes I've systematically posted on the walls of my living space. These quotes are quotes of encouragement, motivation, and inspiration. I assert that every parent should speak positive affirmations to their sons everyday. These quotes remind him of his value, his importance, and his potential. I have included 15 positive affirmations that should be quoted weekly by our sons. These affirmations are powerful and build confidence.

1. I am smart.
2. I can do whatever I focus my mind on.
3. I am a awesome person.
4. I am a learner.
5. I am special.
6. I am worthy.
7. I enjoy learning.
8. I believe in my abilities.
9. I am creative.
10. I learn from my mistakes.
11. I do my best
12. I am kind, generous and loving.
13. I complete my work on time.
14. I am handsome.
15. I believe in my dreams.

These are just a few of the positive affirmations that have carried me through life. These are also affirmations that I use in my mentoring sessions with young boys. With the constant barrage of negative stereotypes casted on our sons, these affirmations can be used to reinforce the positive over the negative.

Chapter 8 :"It Will Take A Village"

As I pen this chapter the 2014 trial of Michael Dunn has just ended with him being found guilty of first degree murder in the shooting death of Jordan Davis. Michael Dunn, a white man living in Florida was on trial for the shooting death of teenager Jordan Davis. Davis and three friends were approached by Dunn in November 2012 after Dunn asked the teenagers to turn their music down at Florida gas station. It is believed that an argument ensued, subsequently with Dunn pulling his son and firing up to ten rounds into the teenager's car. Michael Dunn contended that young Jordan Davis had a shotgun in his car, this mysterious shotgun was never found by the authorities. Dunn, after firing ten shots into Davis's car never called the authorities. This was a case of "shoot first and ask questions last." The outcome of Dunn's trial sent shockwaves through the country. Dunn was found guilty of three counts of second-degree attempted murder, but was not found guilty initially of first degree murder in the death of Jordan Davis.

Not only has this case caused many to question the use of deadly force, it has also caused many to ask the question, "Does white fear matter more than black lives?" In Chapter 2 we discussed the devaluation of our sons in this country. It's safe to say that the more things change, the more they actually stay the same. When these type of cases happen it leaves a bitter taste in the mouths of African Americans, or those that have become far too familiar with dealing with a justice system that never seems to tilt in their favor. Though Dunn is going to prison, this terrible act still brings questions to the forefront. Many questioned if true justice would ever be served, considering that Florida is no stranger to unfair trials. 2013 witnessed the acquittal of George Zimmerman in the shooting death of Trayvon Martin. "According to the criminal justice system of Florida, you are right to fear African American men, and if you decide to act on that fear with violence, then you stand a good chance of avoiding conviction, on account of a jury that-more likely than not-will sympathize with your fear." Statistics show that in states that have a "Stand Your Ground" law, homicides with a white killer and a black victim are mostly ruled "justifiable". This is a story that's becoming far too familiar in this country. The sad thing is that this has been happening for far too long.

In the early 20th century lynchings were common place. This was the kind of racial terrorism that caused many to fear for their very lives, especially those willing to stand up and speak truth to power. This very fear of black men caused the assassination of Dr. Martin Luther King Jr, Medgar Evans, and many others that were not as famous. Many believe that it has become "open killing season" on our sons, looking at the cases arising daily it is hard to disagree. If the trials of Zimmerman and Dunn tell us anything about America, they tell us that some things never change.

It Takes a Village

In February 2014, President Barack Obama launched an initiative known as "My Brother's Keeper". This initiative was put in place to bolster the lives of young minority boys in this country, or those who are disproportionately affected by crime, poverty, and high prison rates. President Obama in this plan made promises to bring foundations and companies together to perform strategies that will lead to higher graduation rates, and a lower rate of incarceration amongst boys of color. Plans such as this are long overdue. The truth of the matter is this: It takes a valiant effort on the part of everyone to help our young people. While it is admirable that the President has introduced such an initiative, the responsibility falls on the "village" to step up and help create bright futures for our sons. The "village" can be described in a number of ways. The village that I speak of is the network of parents, grandparents, aunties, uncles, cousins, pastors, teachers, mentors, leaders, and all others that have access to young people that need encouragement, motivation, and determination in life.

The village concept is certainly not a foreign concept to those that grew up in eras gone by. There was a time when adults in the community acted as your parents because they had interest in seeing you have a bright future. It seems that over time the village concept has taken a back seat to drug infested neighborhoods, joblessness, and despair. The village was known for instilling discipline and keeping you on the straight and narrow. These were households of encouragement and stability. This beloved village that I speak of can still be seen in some neighborhoods, but is yet lacking in many others. At some point we are called to not just talk about the village of old, but create the village we desire to see. We have to be the change we want to see. The government can only do so much. We must take back our streets, our communities, and our children. This is especially needed in a time when so many of our sons are growing up with no father in the home. There is work to be done. It still takes a village.

The American Dream Redefined

When I was growing up in the 80's and 90's there was often a lot of talk around the American Dream. This mystical notion of an American dream usually dealt with purchasing a home, a car, having children, and owning a dog that roamed inside a white picket fence. These days I feel that the American dream needs to be redefined. It is our job as village elders to define the American dream. For many of our sons it is a dream to just graduate High School and be alive at 18 years old. It is hard to imagine, but it is true. When we redefine the American Dream we give young people permission to dream bigger and reach higher. This means fulfilling the dream of living a healthy life free from the threat of untimely death perpetuated through senseless crime and poverty driven issues. This dream becomes harder to actualize when so may of our sons are being lost to the criminal justice system. It is the job of the village to prepare our boys for economic self-sufficiency. This means using every resource we have to prepare our sons for a bright future. A bright future is one that includes more than just being alive at 18. We have to be able to give hope that carries over into their lives. The reality is when we look at statistics the future looks bleak. These days even the children of middle class African Americans are likely to deal with downward mobility in today's economic landscape. For many the concept of an "American Dream" is nothing more than a myth. It is a myth that seems to keep many people on a constant hamster wheel of failed dreams and complacency. This is why it is of great importance that we continue to teach and develop the minds of our sons. Even if we never experience the "American Dream", we can still have a dream worth living. Let's redefine the dream....

<u>Action Plan</u>

It would be a great disservice to produce a work about saving our boys and not have a workable, relatable, and applicable plan in action. This is the very reason in 2013 I became co-founder of "Sons of Sons" Rites of Passage program. This program was instituted to help guide young African American boys into manhood. This program values itself on teaching self-awareness to African American boys ages 12-18. Programs like this are important because statistically African American males are at a higher risk of unemployment, imprisonment, poverty, murder, and a host of other issues that affect their quality of life. As a way of intervention this program was designed to affirm the participants while engaging them. Sons of Sons is preparing young boys for a bright future. This is done by studying historical African American figures, performing achievement activities, personal story telling, and Biblical study time. I believe these type of programs are needed in our communities to help foster life success in the lives of our sons. There is yet work to be done. Let's get going....

Work To Do

Recently there has been a renewed interest on the subject of fatherless children in the black community. It does not take long before the discussion of fatherless boys instantly turns to one on prison population rates, crime rates, and finger pointing. The truth of the matter is that fatherless sons are a pertinent issue in today's society. The numbers surrounding this issue are staggering. There was a 2014 article printed in the Huffington Post entitled, "Fatherless Black Boys: Do You Really Care or Nah?" This article really hit home for those that really care and have an interest in seeing black boys succeed.

This article delved into the incident surrounding a news journalist being fired after suggesting that black boys that had recently committed a heinous crime had to be fatherless. The journalist exact words were, "The underlining cause for all of this, of course, is young black men growing up without fathers." He then goes on to say that it's a shame that those in the media refuse to touch this critical subject. The journalist was suspended for making these comments, but I feel these statements need to be dissected and examined to discover if there is any truth to them. Instantly some will say that he was dead wrong. Others would probably agree with the journalist. Some in the black community felt that the journalist was out of place and out of touch, seeing that he was white and speaking on an issue that deals with African Americans. Well, let's examine the numbers and come to our own conclusions. In 2012, The Root published an article entitled "72 Percent of African American Children Born To Unwed Mothers." As you can imagine, this article created much uproar. This article really struck a nerve because the numbers are staggering, and unbelievable to many. According to www.children-ourinvestment.org, homes without fathers ultimately affect children in numerous tragic ways:

-63% of youth suicides are from fatherless homes

-90% of all homeless and runaway children are from fatherless homes

-85% of all children who show behavior disorders came from fatherless homes

-80% of rapist with anger problems came from fatherless homes

-71% of all high school dropouts came from fatherless homes

-75% of all adolescent patients in chemical-abuse centers from fatherless homes

-85% of all youth in prison come from fatherless homes

The crippling reality is that these aforementioned numbers apply to African American homes in high numbers. "Compared with the 72 percent in our communities, 17 percent of Asians, 29 percent of whites, 53 percent of Hispanics, and 66 percent of Native Americans were born to unwed mothers in 2008, the most recent year for which government figures were available. These numbers should cause alarm for us all. This is a major problem. While there are those in this country that use these numbers to further throw degradation on black people, those of us that care about our children can use these numbers to begin attacking the problem. The effects of fatherless sons are seen throughout this country, especially in lower-income communities. These issues must be addressed. The village is needed....

The Village Against Police Brutality

It is not possible to write a book centered around the African American male and not address the rampant increase of brutality against our young men. In Chapter 1, we included a detailed list of African American males that have been slaughtered at the hands of police officers, those sworn to protect and serve. As I pen these lines the country has just witnessed another case of brutal force and brutality on a young African American male by police. Mike Brown, an 18 year old teenager was tragically killed by multiple gunshots in his hometown of Ferguson, Missouri. The killing of Brown instantly sparked and ignited protest in the small town of Ferguson. This scene, like many others has become all too familiar to people of color. This latest tragedy for many has caused people to question the very way police officers perform their jobs. Immediately following the murder of Brown the police department moved into what could be described as a militarization posture against protestors, using tanks, tear gas, and intimidation tactics on the protestors. This scene became very reminiscent of those witnessed in the 50's and 60's.

This murder has caused many to take their anger and frustrations to social media platforms such as Facebook, Twitter, Instagram, and other activism blogs. Brown's lifeless body was left in the middle of the street for at least four hours before it was removed. Brown's death has served as a blatant reminder of the challenges faced by our boys, just for being black. If an unarmed teen can be executed in broad daylight by police, what message does that send to our young boys? For many, police are seen as the actual aggressors instead of the protecting force they should be; which was evidenced by the way the department treated this tragedy. This case has witnessed police officers become soldiers with an "us against the community" mentality. This is truly sad. Some would like to say that race relations have improved in this country, others assert that race relations have gone backwards. I believe the latter. Mike Brown has become another trophy on the wall of an overzealous police officer. The numbers begin to tell the story of Ferguson, Missouri police department. The city has 53 officers, with only 3 of those officers being black. "The largely white force stops black residents far out of proportion to their population, according to statistics kept by the state attorney general. Blacks account for 86 percent of the arrest after those stops.

It is quite apparent that there is a major problem in this city. The sad thing is that these acts of brutality on our sons are increasing. In Chapter 1, I outlined several names of those killed by police officers even though they were unarmed. As I write these words 4 unarmed black men have been killed in a one month span. Eric Garner on July 17, 2014, John Crawford on August 5th, 2014, Ezell Ford on August 11th, 2014, and Michael Brown on August 9th, 2014. These four names are just four on a long list of others that could be named. There is an epidemic of death that seems to have our sons' name on it. This is exactly why the village is needed. The village is needed now more than ever, needed to rise up and let their voices be heard.

What Can We Do

As we have openly witnessed through the media and other outlets, police brutality is running rampant. Our sons are being gunned down like animals in this country. It is hard to get respect from people that often view you as a criminal before even talking to you. So, the question becomes, "What can we do as citizens to help stop the abuse of our sons at the hand of policemen?" There are several things that we can do to help stop police brutality, but I have proposed 2 things we can focus on instantly:

#1- Expose Actions

We must continue using our cameras and other devices to expose the actions of abuse. The internet can become our ally in broadcasting beatings, harassment, and murder. Most cell phones have cameras these days, let's use them. The world needs to become aware of the mistreatment being passed out by the police.

#2- Continue Voting

This is something we can do for ourselves. Politicians that will not stand with the community against the brutality used against our sons have to be voted out of office. We have to hold our politicians accountable for their silence in the face of injustice. Our communities deserve the total support of the people we have put in office. Let's become the village.

Chapter 9: From Peril to Promise

In previous chapters we have discussed mentoring, education, and creating a solid foundation for our sons. Many will raise issue with the title of this book to be sure. Others will ask if I've lost my mind by even suggesting that black boys can be saved. Some will even assert that those advocating for black boys are simply wasting their time. Over the years I have personally been challenged on my idea that black boys can achieve at a high level. Yes, there are those that believe these boys are worthless and not worth attempting to save. Whenever you attempt to present ways to save our sons many will question if it's even possible. However, there are always those interested in helping to bring out the best in our sons. There are those who can foster growth and creativity in our sons, if we are willing to partner with them. Sometimes looking at the landscape and enormity of the problem is quite daunting and frustrating. The problems facing the black family in general, and black boys in particular are varied. "The Muslims say the solution is separation: the NAACP says its voting power: the Urban League says its educational programs; the government's answer to the crisis is to lock them up and throw away the key." One thing is for sure, the government's solution is certainly not the answer, nor can we allow it to be. It comes down to "value". In an earlier chapter I discussed value and the way our young men are often see as valueless in this country. Our issue has been being able to articulate the problem, but not stepping up to solve the problem. The fact of the matter is "we can all do more". This is a matter that has to be solved by all of us.

While we adults are still fighting over superficial and material things our sons are suffering like never before. We have boys that cannot read, boys that cannot do third grade level mathematics, boys that cannot write a clear sentence, and boys that feel they have no destiny or purpose. This is a problem. If our sons are going to go from peril to promise we have much work to do..

<u>Don't Talk About It, Be About It</u>

Over the years I have learned that there are those that love to talk a good game, while refusing to actually get in the game. It will take more than talk to save a generation of young boys. It will take all hands on deck to perform such a critical task. In a previous Chapter I outlined the importance of mentoring as one of the major tools of effecting the lives of these boys. Mentoring will always be critical in the struggle to steer our sons in the right direction. It's time to do more than "talk a good game". I shall never forget mentoring and speaking to a group of young boys at a local Atlanta summer camp. The mentoring session quickly took a turn for me after a seven year old confessed that the most important thing in his neighborhood was having a gun and being able to shoot someone. You can imagine my reaction as I heard such distressful words coming from a young, shy, baby faced seven year old. If the importance of saving our sons was not yet clear in my mind, it certainly became clear at that point. In this young boy's face I was able to hear a cry for help, a cry for belonging, a cry for life. While knowing the many systemic issues facing our communities, it is still disheartening to see many of our boys going through the things they are going through. Our focus and attention has to be on the ever growing issues they face. Don't just talk a good game....

Let's Strategize

Now that we have taken several chapters to articulate the problems, it's time to talk about solutions. I am a firm believer in using many and varied strategies to reach young boys. While I personally ascribe to a one-on-one mentoring model, I agree that there are others strategies that may be just as important. In this chapter I will lay out strategies that have been proposed by myself and others to help our sons. In a recent 2013 Ebony Magazine Special Report, an article entitled "10 Things Parents Can Do For Their Sons" was released. Let's take a look at this list.

1. Don't put a television in his room. Researchers have found a television in the room can impede a child's intellectual and academic development.
2. Closely monitor his usage of the computer, cell phone and the music he is listening to. Make sure all media content is age appropriate.
3. Talk to him as much as possible, beginning in the womb.

4. Involve him in music and arts programs, in addition to sports.
5. Feed him a healthy breakfast every morning.
6. Make sure he gets a good night's sleep every night.
7. As much as you can, sign him up for outside academic programs and tutoring.
8. Particularly as he moves into adolescence, help him find an outside activity he loves that will help him learn discipline and how to self-regulate his behavior.
9. Do as much as you can to instill a love of reading. Read aloud to him and, as he gets older, read the same books so that you can discuss them with him.
10. Keep him engaged and stimulated during the summer, signing him up for camps and fun programs. If you can't afford them, design a fun summer curriculum for him yourself.

I found these 10 points to be very informative and practical. This is a list that can be implemented by parents immediately.

<u>It Starts At Home</u>

In order to go from peril to promise there are things that must be done at home. No longer can we expect teachers to instill all the lessons we should be instilling at home. You will always be your child's first mentor. In a previous chapter we discussed the epidemic of boys failing in the area of reading by third grade. This should cause great alarm for us all. The statistics should impact us because they are disturbing. Studies show that fewer than 50 percent of black males complete high school in many states. Education does not begin at school; it has to begin at home. Adults are responsible for helping to turn these failing trajectories around that we are witnessing. Education is very pivotal in the success of our sons. Below is a list of additional things we can start doing and implementing:

1. Parents and mentors have to make sure boys are reading earlier and more often.

2. Parents must invest in additional learning materials that can help enhance the child.

3. Parents should research and question any medication or diagnosis of learning disorders diagnosed for their son.

4. Parents and mentors have to promote healthy and positive friendships for boys.

4. Parents must develop strong relationships with their son's teachers.

5. Parents have to continue stressing the importance of education, technology, and good character with their son.

State of Emergency: Act Now

To say we need to act now would be an understatement. The time for talking and debating things that don't matter is over. We are in a serious state of emergency and its time to move. All of us have to start mentoring, reaching out, and speaking life into our sons. We can save our sons- the power is in our hands. Get busy...

"I have only just a minute, only 60 seconds in it,
Forced upon me, can't refuse it,
Didn't seek it, didn't choose it,
But it's up to me to use it.
I must suffer if I lose it,
Give account if I abuse it,
Just a tiny little minute,
But eternity is in it,.
What are you going to do with your minute?
Benjamin E. Mayes, Former Morehouse President

Bibliography

Lee Habeeb. "The War Against Black Men". www.nationalreview.com/articles/337929/war-against-black-men. Accessed on August 6 2013

Jenee-Desmond-Harris. "Beyond Trayvon: Black and Unarmed". The Root. http://www.theroot.com/multimedia/beyond-trayvon-black-andunarmed. Accessed on August 8, 2013

Hawkins, D.F., Lamb, J.H., Lauritsen, J.L., &Cothern, L. (2000). "Race, ethnicity, and serious and violent juvenile offending. National Criminal Justice Reference Service, Washington DC: Department of United States Justice

Kunjufu, J. (2001). State of Emergency: We Must Save African American Males. Chicago: African American Images

Shanelle Matthews. The Devaluation of Black Life. http://www.racialicious.com/2012/13/21/the-devaluation-of0black-life/. Accessed on August, 19, 2013

Woodson, Carter G. The Mis-Education of the Negro. Reprint ed. EWorld Inc., 1933

Timothy M. Smeeding, "The Gap Between the Rich and Poor: A cross National Perspective For Why

Inequality Matters and What Policy Can Do to Alleviate It" (March 2001), "Wealth Inequality in the United States Leads the World and the Gap Here Is Widening, "Twentieth Century Fund, 1995

Robert Balfantz, "Urban High Schools and Racial Disparities in Holding Power, "Working Power, 2003

R.J. Skiba, R.S. Michael, A.C. Nardo, and R. Peterson: The Color of Discipline: Sources of Racial and Gender Disproportionately in School Punishment. Urban Review, 2000

DeShuna Spencer. "Throwback: Tim King of Urban Prep Discusses What It Means to Be 100 Percent. http://www.empowermagazine.com/tim-king-of-urban-prep-discusses-being-100-percent/ Accessed on August 23, 2013

Walter E. Williams. "Should Black People Tolerate This?" http://townhall.com/columnist/Walterewilliams/2012/05/23/should-black-people-tolerate-this/page/full. Assessed on August 23, 2013

Annie Murphy Paul. "Why Third Grade is So Important: The Matthew Effect. www.ideas.time.com/2012/09/26/why-third-grade-is-so-important-in-the-matthew-effect/ Accessed on September 9, 2013

Tamika Thompson. "Fact Sheet: Outcomes for Young, Black Men." www.pbs.org/wnet/tavissmiley/tsr/too-important-to-fail/fact-sheet-outcomes-for-young-blackmen. Accessed on September 16, 2013

Dr. Kunjufu. "Understanding Black Male Learning Styles Critical to Academic Success." http://newswirehouston.com/2011/02/08/only-12-of-black-boys-are-on-grade-level/. Accessed on September 16, 2013

Dan Shipley. The Daily Green. www.thedailygreen.com/environmental-news. Accessed on September 26, 2013

Trelease, J. (2001). Read-Aloud Handbook (5th ed.). New York: Viking-Penguin

Tio Hardiman. African-American Males Facing Serious Challenges. www.huffingtonpost.com/tio-hardiman. Retrieved on Jan.10 2014

"What Challenges Are Boys Facing and What Opportunities Exist to Address those Challenges? www.aspe.hhs.gov/hsp/08/Boys/Findings1/brief.shtm

Akbar, Naim. Visions for Black Men. Tallahassee: Mind Productions & Associates, 1992.

Kunjufu J. (2005) "Keeping Black Boys Out of Special Education. Chicago: African American Images

Dubois, D and Karcher, M. (2005). The Handbook of Youth Mentorsing. Sage Publications. Thousand Oaks, CA.

Dellum Commission. (2006). A Way Out: Creating Partners for our Nation's Prosperity by Expanding Life Paths of Youth Men of Color: Final Report. Joint Center for Political and Economic Studies, Washington, D.C.

Fountain, D.L., and Arbreton, A. 1999. "The Cost of Mentoring." In J.B. Crossman (Ed.), Contemporary Issues in Mentoring, 48-65. Philadelphia: Public/Rrivate Ventures

Jamelle Bovie. "Michael Dun Trial: White Fear Matters More Than Black Lives." www.dailybeast.com. Retrieved on Feb. 16, 2014

Kelsey Minor. Fatherless Black Boys: Do you really care or nah?. Posted: 07/17/2014. www.huffingtonpost.com. Accessed on 08/09/2014

Nsenga Burton. "72 Percent of African American Children Born to Unwed Mothers". www.theroot.com. Accessed on 08/09/2014

The New York Times. Editorial Board. "The Death of Michael Brown", Racial History Behind the Ferguson Protests. Accessed Aug 12, 2014

Jim Holley. "Sound the Trmphet Again: Saving Our Black Boys in American." www.cbn.com. Accessed on August 24, 2014

Nick Chiles. 'Saving Our Sons: Ebony Magazine Special Report. www.mybrownbaby.com. Accessed on August 24, 2014

About The Author

O'nae Chatman was raised in a godly home by a loving grandmother that cared for him from the time of his birth in 1982. O'nae grew up in a small town in Mississippi. Growing up in a small town taught him the value of hard work and education. It was in college that O'nae's life would forever be changed. O'nae enrolled at the University of Phoenix and graduated with honors. O'nae then enrolled at the Interdenominational Theological Center-Morehouse School of Religion in Atlanta Ga where he would earn a Masters Degree in Christian Education, while making the Dean's List the entirety of the program. O'nae plans to start Doctoral Studies in the fall of 2015. O'nae's love and passion for youth and youth ministry has earned him mentor awards, as well as receiving many other awards for service to the community at large. O'nae has been blessed to travel the country speaking to groups of all ages. He is a very sought after speaker. He speaks on the the topics of youth empowerment, leadership, love, and self development. He has addressed audiences for countless church organizations, community outreach organizations, and has even been invited to speak on college campuses. O'nae is an author of two books and has coached others in the area of writing and leadership development. O'nae's first book "Flesh vs Spirit" in which he wrote at the tender age of 24 was released in the fall of 2012, garnering instant regional success. O'nae lives by the philosophy that every moment is a teachable moment if we take the time to apply ourselves. O'nae has been credited with helping the lives of many young people through preaching, teaching, motivational speaking, and encouragement through education and mentoring. O'nae's story is a testament that even those born in small towns can be great when they allow God to work through them. Life is what you make it. The choice is yours!!!

Contact Info: onae.chatman@gmail.com

Made in the USA
Middletown, DE
22 June 2022